It Came From BENEATH THE PEW

Rob Suggs

INTERVARSITY PRESS
DOWNERS GROVE, ILLINOIS 60515

InterVarsity Press is the book-publishing division of InterVarsity Christian Fellowship, a student movement active on campus at hundreds of universities, colleges and schools of nursing. For information about local and regional activities, write Public Relations Dept., InterVarsity Christian Fellowship, 6400 Schroeder Rd., P.O. Box 7895, Madison, WI 53707-7895.

Distributed in Canada through InterVarsity Press, 860 Denison St., Unit 3, Markham, Ontario L3R 4H1, Canada.

Cover illustration: Rob Suggs

ISBN 0-8308-1261-X
Library of Congress Catalog Card Number: 89-15365

Printed in the United States of America ∞

17	16	15	14	13	12	11	10	9	8	7	6	5	4	3	2	1
99	98	97	96	95	94	93	92	91	90	89						

FOR MOM AND DAD

FOR LETTING ME COLOR OUTSIDE THE LINES

Foreword

It Came from Beneath the Pew is Rob Suggs's gift of humor to those who sometimes forget that laughter is medicine strong enough to cancel fatigue, cleanse boredom and lighten the heaviness we thought might crush us. For years Rob Suggs's cartoons have stopped me from living under such self-inflicted heaviness and have reminded me that while I can still laugh, I am able to touch the world with hope. There is an old proverb that says, "Laugh and the world laughs with you, weep and you weep alone!" Our moroseness is only as severe as our willingness to live in it. Misery is a self-inflicted option, as is laughter. Time and time again, I have been encouraged to quit taking myself so seriously when I meet Suggs's cartoons at unexpected moments in magazines and journals.

Suggs's humor is for those who are healthy enough to laugh at themselves. He is not a cartoonist for the squeamish or those who have declared with acid churchmanship, "Christianity is no laughing matter." The truth is, his cartoons remind us that the church always contains, within its thousands of relationships, places where laughing is a sound response. This book comes from "beneath the pew," as it suggests. It is a summons to those who "sit in pew" to laugh. So let us gather in joy, laughing not at the sacred, but the faults and foibles of our own frailties. Our laughter will not make us stronger, but it will channel his grace into human understanding. And we will bless the laughter by which he wraps his grace in joy! And, as one of the martyrs reminds us, joy is the most infallible proof of the presence of God. Thanks, Rob Suggs, for "drawing" us into joy.

Calvin Miller
Omaha, Nebraska

CLIFTON'S TATTOO WAS BIBLICALLY ACCURATE, AND MADE A FINE CONVERSATION PIECE AS WELL.

The Next Trend: Christian Horror

AGGRESSIVE OUTREACH

PAUL'S THIRD MISSIONARY JOURNEY BEGINS

Suggs

C.S. LEWIS, A NARNIAN, AND ITS AGENT

JOHN CALVIN INVENTS PREDESTINATION

THE CELEBRATED ROLLER USHERS OF THIRD CHURCH

A PROUD DAY: PASTOR BOB IS AWARDED HIS FIRST GARGOYLE.

WHEN BIBLE TRANSLATIONS GET OUT OF HAND

Why the Sabbath isn't on Monday

NEW in the Church Gift Shop!

A delightful boutique found in the Narthex...Stop by and pick up a souvenir this Sunday!

KEEP YOUR CAR COOL WHILE SHARING A SCRIPTURAL INSIGHT SURE TO BE APPRECIATED BY THE WHOLE PARKING LOT WITH A **REV. ROWDY AUTO SHADE.** LET OUR PASTOR HELP YOU BLOCK SUN AND SIN!

REV. ROWDY SAYS... YOU THINK IT'S HOT IN HERE... JUST WAIT BUDDY! IF

...AND FOR THE BACK, HOW ABOUT A **REV. ROWDY REAR WINDOW CLINGER?** THIS 5" FACSIMILE OF OUR OWN PASTOR WILL ENCOURAGE THOSE BEHIND YOU IN TRAFFIC TO CONSIDER BIBLICAL ALTERNATIVES TO TAILGATING.

Suggs

ACCOMPANIMENT TAPES FOR PREACHING

GREAT HOUNDS OF THE OLD TESTAMENT

MOSES' DOG "BULLRUSH," WHO HELPED FIND THE PROMISED LAND.

Bible Characters *and their* NICKNAMES!

"HOLY" MOSES   "JUMPIN'" JEHOSHAPHAT   "GRIZZLY" ADAM

TAG TEAM WITNESSING

A PASTOR AND HIS COUNSELING LIBRARY

BOOT CAMP FOR YOUTH MINISTERS

GREETING CARDS OF THE EARLY CHURCH

"I DON'T THINK THEY WANT A PASTORAL VISIT."

SINGLES MINISTRY →

EARLY CHURCH MAIL

A SUDDEN ATTACK OF "PREACHER'S BLOCK"

ARCHAEOLOGISTS UNEARTH THE LONG LOST "DEAD SEA CARTOONS"

HOT SERMONS

JOHN THE BAPTIST POPULARIZES THE "SLAM DUNK"

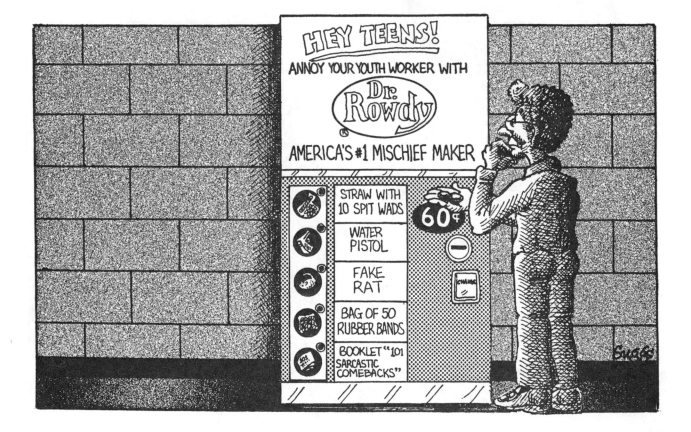

JEREMIAH WAS A BULLFROG

NUMBER ONE PEST OF CHURCH BUILDINGS: THE CHRISTIAN CARTOONIST